REFLECTIONS
FOR
ADVENT

28 November – 24 December 2016

JOANNA COLLICUTT
STEVEN CROFT

with an introduction to Advent
by SAMUEL WELLS

Church House Publishing
Church House
Great Smith Street
London SW1P 3AZ

ISBN 978 0 7151 4741 2

Published 2016 by Church House Publishing
Copyright © The Archbishops' Council 2016

The opinions expressed in this book are those of the
authors and do not necessarily reflect the official policy
of the General Synod or The Archbishops' Council of the
Church of England.

Liturgical editor: Peter Moger
Series editor: Hugh Hillyard-Parker
Designed and typeset by Hugh Hillyard-Parker
Copy edited by: Ros Connelly
Printed by Ashford Colour Press Ltd.

What do you think of *Reflections for Daily Prayer*?

We'd love to hear from you – simply email us at

publishing@churchofengland.org

or write to us at

Church House Publishing, Church House,
Great Smith Street, London SW1P 3AZ.

Visit **www.dailyprayer.org.uk** for more
information on the *Reflections* series, ordering
and subscriptions.

Contents

About *Reflections for Advent*

Based on the *Common Worship Lectionary* readings for Morning Prayer, these daily reflections are designed to refresh and inspire times of personal prayer. The aim is to provide rich, contemporary and engaging insights into Scripture.

Each page lists the Lectionary readings for the day, with the main psalms for that day highlighted in **bold**. The Collect of the day – either the *Common Worship* collect or the shorter additional Collect – is also included.

For those using this book in conjunction with a service of Morning Prayer, the following conventions apply: a psalm printed in parentheses is omitted if it has been used as the opening canticle at that office; a psalm marked with an asterisk may be shortened if desired.

A short reflection is provided on either the Old or New Testament reading. Popular writers, experienced ministers, biblical scholars and theologians have contributed to this series, bringing their own emphases, enthusiasms and approaches to biblical interpretation to bear.

Regular users of Morning Prayer and *Time to Pray* (from *Common Worship: Daily Prayer*) and anyone who follows the Lectionary for their regular Bible reading will benefit from the rich variety of traditions represented in these stimulating and accessible pieces.

This volume also includes both a simple form of *Common Worship: Morning Prayer* (see pp. 34–5) and a short form of Night Prayer – also known as Compline – (see pp. 38–41), particularly for the benefit of those readers who are new to the habit of the Daily Office or for any reader while travelling.

About the authors

Joanna Collicutt is the Karl Jaspers Lecturer in Psychology and Spirituality at Ripon College Cuddesdon and Advisor on the Spiritual Care of Older People for Oxford Diocese. Her professional background is in clinical psychology, but her current area of academic interest is psychology of religion. She also ministers in a West Oxfordshire parish.

Stephen Cottrell is the Bishop of Chelmsford. Before this he was Bishop of Reading and has worked in parishes in London, Chichester, and Huddersfield and as Pastor of Peterborough Cathedral. He is a well-known writer and speaker on evangelism, spirituality and catechesis. His best-selling *How to Pray* (CHP) and *How to Live* (CHP) have recently been reissued.

Steven Croft is the Bishop of Oxford. He was previously Bishop of Sheffield and team leader of Fresh Expressions. He is the author of a number of books including *Leadership: according to the Scriptures* and *The Advent Calendar*, a novel for children and adults.

John Pritchard retired as Bishop of Oxford in 2014. Prior to that he was Bishop of Jarrow, Archdeacon of Canterbury and Warden of Cranmer Hall, Durham. His only ambition was to be a vicar, which he was in Taunton for eight happy years. He enjoys armchair sport, walking, reading, music, theatre and recovering.

Samuel Wells is Vicar of St Martin in the Fields, London, and Visiting Professor of Christian Ethics at King's College, London. He is the author of a number of acclaimed books; his most recent titles are *What Anglicans Believe*, *Crafting Prayers for Public Worship* and *Learning to Dream Again*. He was formerly Dean of the Chapel and Research Professor of Christian Ethics at Duke University, North Carolina.

'Never Mind the Width ...'
– A reflection on the season of Advent

Back in the days when it was common to go into a tailor's shop and ask for yards of cloth for sewing or dressmaking into trousers or skirts or outer garments, people would imitate the proverbial salesperson and say, 'Never mind the quality – feel the width!' In other words, 'Who cares whether the material is the very best fabric? See how much there is of it, for such a bargain price!' It's a parable for what we do to our lives to hide ourselves from the depths of our struggles and sadness and pain. 'Never mind our deepest desires – see how easy it is to occupy ourselves with our most trivial ones! Don't distress yourself about the things that really matter – see how quickly you can get your hands on the things that don't!' It's perfectly possible to turn your whole life into a distraction, a whole enterprise of feeling the width. Maybe that's what you're doing right now.

The Church has a season for helping us set aside our distractions and get profoundly in touch with the powerlessness of waiting. It's called Advent. In Advent we dismantle our elaborate defences, and, for a few weeks, or days, or moments, face up squarely to our deepest yearnings, our unresolved longings and our rawest needs. But Advent is also about a confidence deeper than our needs, a hope more far-reaching than our desires, a future more comprehensive than our most poignant yearnings.

In our self-protection we habitually say to ourselves, to one another, and even to God, 'Never mind the quality, feel the width. Let's just make ourselves busy and perhaps we'll forget about all the tricky stuff.' In Advent, God says to us, 'Never mind the width. Your life isn't about quantity of activity or length of days. Let go of the width. Feel the depth.'

The answer to the agony of waiting isn't width. It's depth. Just for once, in this Advent season, feel the depth of your life, and look into the deep heart of God. Look at your hands. Think of the Father's hands that made the world; think of the Son's hands and the nail-marks in the centre of them; think of the Spirit's hands, and realize they're the hands you're looking at right now. Look at your feet. These are feet that can walk with others in their pain; these are feet that can dance to the beat of God's heart; these are feet that can run with the wind of God's Spirit.

Feel your skin. Skin that Christ took on; skin that can touch the tender suffering of another; skin that's made to protect and stretch the boundary of your being. Feel the depth.

Advent says, 'Yes, you're hungry. Yes, you long for fulfilment and resolution and completion and consummation. Yes, you're aching all over; yes, if you stopped your incessant activity and paused for one second to look in the mirror, you'd be sobbing with disappointed dreams and deflated desires and unmet longings and dashed aspirations. Yes, life hasn't turned out as you trusted it would; yes, it feels like everyone else has it easier than you; yes, it's sometimes impossible to find the patience to keep going; yes, you feel that if for one moment you admitted your grief, it would crush you and incapacitate you and disable you from functioning in any respectable and grown-up way.' Advent gets to the bottom of our waiting.

But Advent doesn't stop there. Advent goes under and around our waiting. Advent also says, gently, cherishingly and tenderly, 'No. No, this isn't the way the story ends. No, God isn't ignoring you or punishing you. No, this isn't God's last word on the matter. No, God hasn't finished with you. No, this groaning, this aching, this yearning won't be your eternal condition. God came in Christ to be with you, to groan with your groaning, to ache with your aching, to yearn with your yearning. God in Christ suffered on the cross to show you a yearning that is greater even than your yearning, a grieving that is greater even than your grieving, a longing that is greater even than your longing. A yearning and a longing *for you*. Christ rose from the dead to show you how the story ends, that all your pain and agony and tears will be taken up into glory, that all your sadness will be made beautiful and all your waiting will be rewarded. Christ ascended into heaven to show you that you'll spend eternity with God, that your hunger will be met in God's banquet, that everything you long for will be exceeded and overwhelmed in the glory of the presence of God, and that when you see the marks in Christ's hands and the Father's broken heart, you'll finally realize how achingly, convulsingly hungry God has always been for you.'

Just for once this Advent, dare to feel the depth. Never mind the width. If you're tired of waiting, go deeper. Feel the deep texture of life. Eternal life isn't an infinitely extended version of what we have now: it's a deeper version of what we have now. If you want a glimpse of eternal life, even amid the sadness and the longing of waiting, go deeper.

Remember all those people you were envious of and who seemed to have everything you didn't have? Go deeper and see who they really are and what they truly long for, and feel your jealousy begin to melt into compassion. Go deeper into your fears and come out of the bottom of them, and let your hatred become hope. Go deeper into your loneliness and make a companion of the truth you find there. Feel the wonder of your createdness, sense the unlikely mystery of your being here at all. And receive all the rest as a bonus, a gift, a blessing.

Advent isn't an escape. It's an encounter with the time that's deeper than our time, a time we call eternal life. It's a discovery of a longing that's deeper than our longing, the longing we call God's waiting for us. It's an experience deep down and, through the bottom of our experience, a place where grief is no longer isolating but companionable, where alienating hurt becomes tender wisdom, where unfulfilled longing becomes the sculpting of a greater hole for grace.

It's hard to do Advent all year round. It's almost easier to be left alone in our waiting. But just this once, this Advent, take the risk on God that God's taken on you. Feel the quality. Feel the depth. Go deeper and keep digging. Keep digging until you find you've dug deep into the heart of God.

Samuel Wells

The importance of daily prayer

Daily prayer is a way of sustaining that most special of all relationships. It helps if we want to pray, but it can be sufficient to want to want to pray, or even to want to want to want to pray! The direction of the heart is what matters, not its achievements. Gradually we are shaped and changed by the practice of daily prayer. Apprentices in prayer never graduate, but we become a little bit more the people God wants us to be.

Prayer isn't a technique; it's a relationship, and it starts in the most ordinary, instinctive reactions to everyday life:

- **Gratitude**: good things are always happening to us, however small.
- **Wonder**: we often see amazing things in nature and in people but pass them by.
- **Need**: we bump into scores of needs every day.
- **Sorrow**: we mess up.

Prayer is taking those instincts and stretching them out before God. The rules then are: start small, stay natural, be honest.

Here are four ways of putting some structure around daily prayer.

1 **The Quiet Time**. This is the classic way of reading a passage of the Bible, using Bible reading reflections like those in this book, and then praying naturally about the way the passage has struck you, taking to God the questions, resolutions, hopes, fears and other responses that have arisen within you.

2 **The Daily Office**. This is a structured way of reading Scripture and psalms, and praying for individuals, the world, the day ahead, etc. It keeps us anchored in the Lectionary, the basic reading of the Church, and so ensures that we engage with the breadth of Scripture, rather than just with our favourite passages. It also puts us in living touch with countless others around the world who are doing something similar. There is a simple form of Morning Prayer on pages 34–5 and a form of Night Prayer (Compline) on pages 38–41. Fuller forms can be found in *Common Worship: Daily Prayer*.

3 **Holy Reading**. Also known as *Lectio Divina*, this is a tried and trusted way of feeding and meditating on the Bible, described more fully on pages 8–9 of this book. In essence, here is how it is done:

- *Read:* Read the passage slowly until a phrase catches your attention.
- *Reflect:* Chew the phrase carefully, drawing the goodness out of it.
- *Respond:* Pray about the thoughts and feelings that have surfaced in you.
- *Rest:* You may want to rest in silence for a while.
- *Repeat:* Carry on with the passage …

4 **Silence**. In our distracted culture some people are drawn more to silence than to words. This will involve *centring* (hunkering down), *focusing* on a short biblical phrase (such as 'Come, Holy Spirit'), *waiting* (repeating the phrase as necessary), and *ending* (perhaps with the Lord's Prayer). The length of time is irrelevant.

There are, of course, as many ways of praying as there are people to pray. There are no right or wrong ways to pray. 'Pray as you can, not as you can't', is wise advice. The most important thing is to make sure there is sufficient structure to keep prayer going when it's a struggle as well as when it's a joy. Prayer is too important to leave to chance.

+John Pritchard

Lectio Divina – a way of reading the Bible

Lectio Divina is a contemplative way of reading the Bible. It dates back to the early centuries of the Christian Church and was established as a monastic practice by Benedict in the sixth century. It is a way of praying the Scriptures that leads us deeper into God's word. We slow down. We read a short passage more than once. We chew it over slowly and carefully. We savour it. Scripture begins to speak to us in a new way. It speaks to us personally, and aids that union we have with God through Christ, who is himself the Living Word.

Make sure you are sitting comfortably. Breathe slowly and deeply. Ask God to speak to you through the passage that you are about to read.

This way of praying starts with our silence. We often make the mistake of thinking prayer is about what we say to God. It is actually the other way round. God wants to speak to us. He will do this through the Scriptures. So don't worry about what to say. Don't worry if nothing jumps out at you at first. God is patient. He will wait for the opportunity to get in. He will give you a word and lead you to understand its meaning for you today.

First reading: Listen

As you read the passage listen for a word or phrase that attracts you. Allow it to arise from the passage as if it is God's word for you today. Sit in silence repeating the word or phrase in your head.

Then say the word or phrase aloud.

Second reading: Ponder

As you read the passage again, ask how this word or phrase speaks to your life and why it has connected with you. Ponder it carefully. Don't worry if you get distracted – it may be part of your response to offer to God. Sit in silence and then frame a single sentence that begins to say aloud what this word or phrase says to you.

Third reading: Pray

As you read the passage for the last time, ask what Christ is calling from you. What is it that you need to do or consider or relinquish or take on as a result of what God is saying to you in this word or phrase? In the silence that follows the reading, pray for the grace of the Spirit to plant this word in your heart.

If you are in a group, talk for a few minutes and pray with each other.

If you are on your own, speak your prayer to God either aloud or in the silence of your heart.

If there is time, you may even want to read the passage a fourth time, and then end with the same silence before God with which you began.

+Stephen Cottrell

Monday 28 November

Revelation 19

'I heard what seemed to be the loud voice of a great multitude' (v.1)

The Church's year begins with a series of extraordinarily challenging readings from the book of Revelation of John. Advent is the time to wake from sleep. Revelation speaks into our torpor with the action of a cold shower on an early winter's morning: bracing – even painful; disorientating yet forcing us into a new perspective; and ultimately fitting us for action in the world. John is a mysterious figure and he has left us a deeply mysterious document. It is written according to literary rules and conventions that would have told the first Jewish-Christian readers that he was a prophet who wanted to communicate an alternative heavenly perspective on the social, moral and political situation in which they found themselves.

Yet behind the document lies what we might now call a mystical experience. The irony of such experiences is that they are beyond language, but the visionary nevertheless feels compelled to try and communicate what has been seen and heard. Words will not do; yet words are all we have. This is why the phrase 'what seemed to be' is so important. It translates a single Greek word, *hōs*, which simply means 'as if'. Throughout his book John is saying 'it was as if'. He brings the stuff of his own psychology together with images familiar in his culture (for example, the white horse of v.11 draws on Roman iconography of military triumph), and with them paints a picture of his cataclysmic transcendent experience and the vital truths that have been revealed to him through it. We must remember this if we are to make any sense of these readings.

COLLECT

Almighty God,
give us grace to cast away the works of darkness
and to put on the armour of light,
now in the time of this mortal life,
in which your Son Jesus Christ came to us in great humility;
that on the last day,
when he shall come again in his glorious majesty
    to judge the living and the dead,
we may rise to the life immortal;
through him who is alive and reigns with you,
in the unity of the Holy Spirit,
one God, now and for ever.

| *Reflection by* **Joanna Collicutt**

Revelation 20

'Death and Hades gave up the dead that were in them' (v.13)

John's vision is about a heavenly reality that is at odds with the values of his world and a future reality that is at odds with his time, as it is with ours. The reality of the ultimate judgement has been revealed to him and, despite imagery that might perplex and disturb our modern minds, it is fundamentally a vision of hope.

The rider of the white horse from yesterday's reading is Jesus himself, described in messianic images drawn from Exodus 15 and Isaiah 63, who comes to judge the world with truth and fairness. This is a world where the weak and poor are neglected, exploited, persecuted and even murdered on account of the self-interest of those in more powerful positions. The greed, cruelty, or simple apathy of individuals has fed systemic beasts such as local lynch mobs or mighty Imperial Rome, enabling them to perpetrate outrages on those who stand in their way or speak out against them.

Into this situation rides the warrior-judge Jesus to sentence these perpetrators and vindicate their victims. He knows his good wheat by its spiritual fruit (Matthew 13.30; Galatians 5.22, 23) and his sheep by their works of mercy (Matthew 25.32-46; John 10.27). What's more he seeks out and saves them from dark places that we might think beyond his scope or under his radar – the depths of the sea, and the land of the shades. Yet we should not be surprised, for this is the one who plucked Peter from the waves and called Lazarus from the tomb.

Almighty God,
as your kingdom dawns,
turn us from the darkness of sin to the light of holiness,
that we may be ready to meet you
in our Lord and Saviour, Jesus Christ.

COLLECT

Wednesday 30 November

Andrew the Apostle

Psalms 47, 147.1-12
Ezekiel 47.1-12
or Ecclesiasticus 14.20-end
John 12.20-32

Ezekiel 47.1-12

'... it will be a place for the spreading of nets' (v.10)

Today is the feast of St Andrew, the fisherman and disciple of John the Baptist, who recognized Jesus as the Messiah and introduced his brother Peter to him (John 1.37-41). Later, when he left his nets to follow Jesus, he was assured that his fishing days were not over; his catch would simply be different (Mark 1.17).

The reading is from the divine vision of the prophet Ezekiel, a vision in many ways similar in form to that of John – for example, both have a supernatural guide and interpreter (Ezekiel 40.3), and both gain insight into a heavenly perspective. The difference is that while John sees the last days when the new Jerusalem descends to earth (Revelation 21.2), Ezekiel, writing some 600 years earlier, sees the newly rebuilt temple symbolizing the return of God's presence and favour to Jerusalem after the Babylonian Exile.

Ezekiel writes of living water flowing from the presence of God towards the Dead Sea, water that transforms death to life, that supports not simply fruitful abundance (v.9) but also diversity of kind (v.10). This is a work of recreation reminiscent of Genesis. It is not impossible that, as Jesus walked by Lake Galilee, reflecting on his mission to bring fruitfulness and healing by providing living water (John 4.14) and – more than that – to recreate humanity in all its diversity, he caught sight of men casting their nets and was reminded of Ezekiel's ancient vision. Perhaps in such a moment of joyful insight, he could not help but call out, 'Follow me!'

COLLECT

Almighty God,
who gave such grace to your apostle Saint Andrew
that he readily obeyed the call of your Son Jesus Christ
    and brought his brother with him:
call us by your holy word,
and give us grace to follow you without delay
    and to tell the good news of your kingdom;
through Jesus Christ your Son our Lord,
who is alive and reigns with you,
in the unity of the Holy Spirit,
one God, now and for ever.

Revelation 21.9-21

'... a radiance like a very rare jewel, like jasper' (v.11)

The vision of judgement in Revelation 20 gives way to the new order that God is completing. The bestial systems of the world are built on the whoredom of moral compromise, financial corruption and political exploitation. (John has the Roman Empire in mind, but it is easy to identify some contemporary national and multi-national equivalents.) In stark contrast, the New Jerusalem – the kingdom of God – is presented as a good and faithful wife.

Yet John's detailed description of the New Jerusalem is not of a woman but of a kind of crystal city. The key things to notice are that the city comes from heaven and is thus infused with the heavenly (true) perspective on reality, and that it shines with God's glory like a precious stone (vv.10,11). John has been caught up into radiance.

This experience of dazzling multi-faceted light is a feature of visionaries such as Ezekiel, the writer of the book of Enoch (which dates from the first century BC), and the sixteenth-century Spanish nun Teresa of Ávila, who wrote of it in *The Interior Castle*. We might conclude that it is an aspect of the altered state of consciousness undergone by any mystic. But John's interpretation of the radiance is crucial. The jewels are those loaded on a bride by her husband as a mark of his 'everlasting love' for her (Isaiah 54.8-12) – a kind of eternity ring. She shines with the glory of his eternal presence.

The radiance is the joy of the reunion of lover and beloved.

COLLECT

Almighty God,
give us grace to cast away the works of darkness
and to put on the armour of light,
now in the time of this mortal life,
in which your Son Jesus Christ came to us in great humility;
that on the last day,
when he shall come again in his glorious majesty
to judge the living and the dead,
we may rise to the life immortal;
through him who is alive and reigns with you,
in the unity of the Holy Spirit,
one God, now and for ever.

Reflection by **Joanna Collicutt**   13

Psalms **25**, 26 *or* 17, **19**
Isaiah 44.9-23
Revelation 21.22 – 22.5

Revelation 21.22 – 22.5

'Its gates will never be shut' (21.25)

The Genesis creation narrative is marked by separation: the good ordering of chaos as the sea is divided from the dry land, and the night from the day. Later there is the tragic separation of human beings from their first home in the Garden of Eden, a place of precious jewels (Ezekiel 28.13), housing the tree of life. Along with this comes a distance between God and human beings, who are unable to look directly on the divine glory and live to tell the tale (Exodus 33.20).

Now, however, God is completing the new thing he began in the life and death of Christ, where he 'was reconciling the world to himself' (2 Corinthians 5.19). This reconciliation is marked by the breakdown of all sorts of divisions, beginning with Jesus' open welcome of outsiders and his command to love enemies, climaxing with the tearing of the Temple veil, and continuing with the pouring out of the Spirit on Jew and gentile alike.

John has already seen the end of the sea (21.1), and now he sees the end of the night and a city whose gates are always open. There is no more division between pure and impure, sacred and profane. There is no curse hanging over the peoples of the world, because all nations have found healing in the tree of life. Above all there is no more separation from God, whose eternal presence will not be a light that blinds and destroys but one that brings comfort and illumination after a time of deep darkness.

COLLECT

Almighty God,
give us grace to cast away the works of darkness
and to put on the armour of light,
now in the time of this mortal life,
in which your Son Jesus Christ came to us in great humility;
that on the last day,
when he shall come again in his glorious majesty
    to judge the living and the dead,
we may rise to the life immortal;
through him who is alive and reigns with you,
in the unity of the Holy Spirit,
one God, now and for ever.

Reflection by **Joanna Collicutt**

Psalms **9**, (10) *or* 20, 21, **23**
Isaiah 44.24 – 45.13
Revelation 22.6-end

Revelation 22.6-end

'"Surely I am coming soon." Amen. Come, Lord Jesus!' (v.20)

In the new creation there is no more division and separation. Instead there is aggregation around the Lamb. Jesus is at the centre, and people are judged by their response to him; some move forward to be close, and those who are not known by him fade away into the distance. The gates of the city are open to all, but those who do not know and love Jesus cannot walk through them. This is reminiscent of the story of the prodigal, where the father opens the door to his older son who resolutely remains outside (Luke 15.28).

The fundamental theme of this final section of Revelation, which forms the end of the New Testament as a whole, is the imminent arrival of Jesus. It is depicted so vividly as to give a foretaste of his presence. It speaks hope to those who are – as it were – children crying in the dark, wondering if they have been left alone. Into their darkness comes the sense of a distant light approaching and a sound as if of those sweetest of words, 'It's OK! I'm coming!'

No wonder John fell down in worship at what he had been shown; no wonder he felt compelled to tell what he saw.

Almighty God,
as your kingdom dawns,
turn us from the darkness of sin to the light of holiness,
that we may be ready to meet you
in our Lord and Saviour, Jesus Christ.

COLLECT

Reflection by **Joanna Collicutt**   15

Monday 5 December

1 Thessalonians 1

'... brothers and sisters beloved by God' (v.4)

Paul's first letter to the congregation at Thessalonica (modern-day Thessaloniki in Greece) is one of the earliest documents in the New Testament, dating from around 50 AD. Paul and Silas (Silvanus) had established a Christian community in the town only a few months earlier (Acts 17), and from there they had gone south to Corinth via Athens. So, this was a very young and apparently enthusiastic group of Christians who, thanks to Paul's teaching, was expecting the imminent return of Christ some 20 or so years after his death.

Paul had a natural concern for this fledgling Church, perhaps particularly because it appears to have been made up of people exclusively from the artisan class (he mentions no wealthy educated patrons in this letter), so he sent Timothy to check on them. Timothy returned to report that the group was thriving (1 Thessalonians 3.6), and Paul is writing in response to this good news.

Shining through the letter are Paul's longing to be with these folk (whom he calls his brothers and sisters) and his desire to affirm them. He describes this lowly group as 'chosen', not as a statement of double predestination, but to build up their sense of identity and worth. His agenda throughout the letter is Christian love rather than academic theology. Indeed the whole point of writing seems to be to remind the Thessalonians that they are on his heart and that he is in spirit by their side. Perhaps we should write more letters like this.

COLLECT

O Lord, raise up, we pray, your power
and come among us,
and with great might succour us;
that whereas, through our sins and wickedness
we are grievously hindered
in running the race that is set before us,
your bountiful grace and mercy
may speedily help and deliver us;
through Jesus Christ your Son our Lord,
to whom with you and the Holy Spirit,
be honour and glory, now and for ever.

1 Thessalonians 2.1-12

'... you have become very dear to us' (v.8)

One way of reconnecting with people is to remind them of times spent together. Paul retells the story of his coming to Thessalonica, and emphasizes that this was costly to him (and therefore that the Thessalonians are precious). Immediately before coming to Thessalonica, he and Silas had suffered much at Philippi on account of proclaiming Christ (Acts 16.19-24), yet they pressed on regardless.

Paul perhaps emphasizes his experience of persecution as an act of solidarity with the Thessalonians, who are undergoing hardship on account of having renounced the pagan practices (1.9) that were the bread and butter of social and commercial life in their city. He talks of the stigma he carries from the humiliating punishments he endured at Philippi, pointing out that in God's eyes he is approved and has dignity – as have they. He also emphasizes his credentials as a worker who pays his own way. For pastoral purposes he is being one of them – an early example of his chameleon strategy (1 Corinthians 9.22). Paul is not being hypocritical here; he is merely foregrounding the points he has in common with this particular group of brother and sisters.

Yet he also talks to them as his children using parental language, as someone who has brought them to birth (see Galatians 4.19), nurtured them (v.7), and formed their character (vv.11-12). He is like a father who has been parted from his children, who wants to make sure that they are eating well and living right, and who simply misses them.

Reflection by **Joanna Collicutt** | 7

Wednesday 7 December

Psalms **62,** 63 *or* **34**
Isaiah 47
1 Thessalonians 2.13-end

1 Thessalonians 2.13-end

'For what is our hope...?' (v.19)

The theme of parent–child separation is turned on its head by Paul when he describes himself and Silas as 'orphans' (v.17). This is a nice example of Paul's tendency to play with an idea (almost to do it to death), which is developed in some of his later letters where he plays with ideas such as the law and circumcision.

There are some darker references in this part of the letter – to Satan (v.18) and to the wrath of God that will be poured out on the Judean authorities who persecuted the Palestinian Church (v.16), and in whose employ Paul once was (Acts 7.58; 9.1). These dark references in a letter that is dominated by affection remind us of the context in which the early Church was emerging. There was a sense of oppression by massive forces aimed at its violent destruction, but amidst this, as so vividly depicted in Revelation, a sure hope of imminent liberation and vindication by God. This is why Paul emphasizes the Thessalonians' 'steadfastness of hope' alongside the other Christian virtues of faith and love right at the beginning of his letter (1 Thessalonians 1.3).

The challenge for today's reader is that nearly 2,000 years have passed and our hope is now of ultimate rather than imminent vindication and liberation. In our social democracies we have tried to build systems of justice that safeguard minorities and better reflect the justice of God's kingdom. Yet we still yearn for Christ's coming, and we too must remain steadfast in hope.

COLLECT

O Lord, raise up, we pray, your power
and come among us,
and with great might succour us;
that whereas, through our sins and wickedness
we are grievously hindered
in running the race that is set before us,
your bountiful grace and mercy
may speedily help and deliver us;
through Jesus Christ your Son our Lord,
to whom with you and the Holy Spirit,
be honour and glory, now and for ever.

1 Thessalonians 3

'... love for one another and for all' (v.12)

Paul is like an anxious parent; he is desperate to know how his children in the faith are faring, fearing that though they initially received the gospel with joy, the adversity and persecution they are suffering may have led them to 'fall away' (Mark 4.16–17). When he hears that this is not the case, he is overwhelmed with relief. There is also a suggestion that he is reassured that they are missing him as much as he misses them. His relationships with his congregations were not always easy, and it seems that this could be a source of deep sadness to him. Conversely, when the relationship is going well, he is filled with joy (v.9).

Joy is an emotion that is related to happiness, mirth and pleasure, but is distinct from them. It is partly about *joie de vivre* – life; this is why Paul says he may now 'live' (v.8). But joy is also about reunion after separation. The themes of life and reunion come together in community rejoicing when the prodigal returns (Luke 15.32). Joy expresses the fellowship of community, and a precious project brought to fruition. Through Timothy's report, Paul now feels in renewed fellowship with the people who are his pride and joy.

Joy is the second fruit of the Spirit, following love (Galatians 5.22). There cannot be joy without love, and Paul is swift to turn his attention to this primary Christian virtue (v.12) with a timely reminder that our love should not be only for one another, but for *all*.

Almighty God,
purify our hearts and minds,
that when your Son Jesus Christ comes again as
judge and saviour
we may be ready to receive him,
who is our Lord and our God.

COLLECT

1 Thessalonians 4.1-12

'For God did not call us to impurity but in holiness' (v.7)

The Thessalonian Christians have received the good news of Jesus and experienced the indwelling of the Spirit. Paul is concerned that this shows itself in their lifestyle (a particular concern given that they were gentile converts rather than devout Jews).

The call is to be 'holy' or 'sanctified' (vv.3,4,7). This involves turning away from sins and towards the good. In the first part of his letter to the Romans, Paul states that both Jews and gentiles have sinned, but that their sin takes different forms. He caricatures the Jewish sin as hypocrisy (Romans 2.1-3) and the gentile sin as sexual immorality, which he sees as deeply intertwined with idolatry (Romans 1.18-32). Here he urges his readers to turn from sexual impurity precisely because they have turned away from idols. The way they treat their own bodies and the bodies of others is a measure of the authenticity of their conversion.

However, they are also to turn to something: an increase in love within their community. It is a vulnerable community. In their founder's absence they are to safeguard it, not by defensive hostility towards outsiders, but by becoming self-sufficient and keeping under the radar of the authorities. Again we have the feel of an anxious parent imploring a child to 'keep out of trouble' in order that they might have a chance to grow and flourish unmolested and undistracted. Or perhaps a good shepherd who is committed to leading his flock in right paths.

COLLECT

O Lord, raise up, we pray, your power
and come among us,
and with great might succour us;
that whereas, through our sins and wickedness
we are grievously hindered
in running the race that is set before us,
your bountiful grace and mercy
may speedily help and deliver us;
through Jesus Christ your Son our Lord,
to whom with you and the Holy Spirit,
be honour and glory, now and for ever.

1 Thessalonians 4.13-end

'... so that you may not grieve as others do who have no hope' (v.13)

This passage is surely one of the most misunderstood in the New Testament, feeding strange and weird notions of 'the rapture'. The key thing to understand is that Paul is writing to relatively unsophisticated people for whom he cares deeply, and who are understandably worried about what will happen to their recently deceased loved ones when Christ returns (an event that they are expecting to happen at any moment).

Paul makes his motives for writing abundantly clear in verses 13 and 18, which bookend his account of the return of Christ. His aim is to comfort and encourage these individuals in their situation, not to set out a detailed and developed theology of the end times. As in the rest of the letter, he wants them to keep hoping. Above all, as we have seen, Paul is aware that this marginalized group needs to feel connected – to him, to Christ, and to the loved ones whom they sorely miss.

So, he paints a vivid picture of the triumphant and joyful coming of Christ in which, crucially 'together with them' (v.17), we will be raised up to our true status as God's children and will be with Christ for ever. Perhaps this is a picture that had been revealed to Paul directly, as to John in his apocalypse; perhaps it was part of the tradition he had received (1 Corinthians 15.3). Either way, his deeply compassionate take-home message is that we will not be separated from our faithful loved ones in death.

Almighty God,
purify our hearts and minds,
that when your Son Jesus Christ comes again as
judge and saviour
we may be ready to receive him,
who is our Lord and our God.

COLLECT

Monday 12 December

Psalm **40** *or* **44**
Isaiah 49.14-25
1 Thessalonians 5.1-11

1 Thessalonians 5.1-11

'But since we belong to the day, let us be sober...' (v.8)

Advent is the great antidote to the commercial build-up to Christmas. We live in a culture that is encouraging us, for its own reasons, to overspend, overeat, get drunk often and begin all the celebrations weeks in advance. At this time of year, we may be faced almost daily with a different kind of temptation.

In such a culture, the Christian needs sure defences. We need to remember each morning and evening that we belong to the day and walk in the light. At this time of year more than any other, every night we need to remember the simple injunction to be sober: to stay in control of our minds and our desires. In the quietness of each early morning, we need to remember to buckle on our armour: faith and love and hope – the great virtues, or strengths of Christian character.

Only as we do that will we gain the great lesson and perspective of Advent: the ability to live each day in stability, in the light of eternal truths and eternal destiny. This world will not last forever. Darkness has an ending. We are called to live forever in the light. We are not destined for wrath but for salvation. Whether we are awake or asleep, we may live with him.

COLLECT

O Lord Jesus Christ,
who at your first coming sent your messenger
to prepare your way before you:
grant that the ministers and stewards of your mysteries
may likewise so prepare and make ready your way
by turning the hearts of the disobedient to the wisdom of the just,
that at your second coming to judge the world
we may be found an acceptable people in your sight;
for you are alive and reign with the Father
in the unity of the Holy Spirit,
one God, now and for ever.

Reflection by **Steven Croft**

Psalms **70**, 74 *or* **48**, 52
Isaiah 50
I Thessalonians 5.12-end

1 Thessalonians 5.12-end

'May the God of peace ... sanctify you entirely' (v.23)

At the end of this very early New Testament letter, Paul, Silvanus and Timothy extol the qualities that build up Christians communities. The passage no doubt summarized their own preaching, and its own echoes run through other New Testament epistles.

It's quite hard to catch the sense of some of the verbs in English, but the call here is to continuous actions over a very long period of time, not to single instructions. You will get a sense of this if you read the passage slowly and before every imperative verb insert the words 'keep on ...' – 'Keep on admonishing the idlers, keep on encouraging the faint-hearted, keep on helping the weak, keep on being patient with all of them ...'

The call to build the Church is a long-distance race not a sprint. The call to Christian community is a permanent and holy calling to be family together, a call to love without limit as part of God's holy people.

This is a demanding calling and the first ten verses of our passage set up the final prayer. How can we give this kind of love? We can only love like this with the strength that God supplies. This is what it means to be made holy. The letter ends (almost) with a prayer for holiness and strength in the perspective of Christ's second coming.

God for whom we watch and wait,
you sent John the Baptist to prepare the way of your Son:
give us courage to speak the truth,
to hunger for justice,
and to suffer for the cause of right,
with Jesus Christ our Lord.

COLLECT

Wednesday 14 December

Psalms **75**, 96 *or* **119.57-80**
Isaiah 51.1-8
2 Thessalonians 1

2 Thessalonians 1

'To this end we always pray for you ...' (v.11)

Today we begin a second, very early letter to the same Church from the same authors. How does this second letter relate to the first one? There has been much debate. I find Charles Wanamaker's theory in his commentary attractive: 2 Thessalonians was the first letter to be written on the basis of sketchy reports to Paul on life in Thessalonica. Paul then sent Timothy to follow up this first letter with a visit (1 Thessalonians 3.1-2). Following that visit, Paul wrote 1 Thessalonians with the benefit of much more accurate information about the Church's own situation and belief.

Whatever the order of the letters, the background of 2 Thessalonians is growing faith and love (v.3) against a background of persecution and affliction (v.4). The greater the suffering of the Church down the ages, the more eternal destiny and the end times come into focus in the life of the Church. Here Paul, Silvanus and Timothy deploy teaching about the end times and eternal judgement to strengthen the Church in times of suffering. God is able to use even times of difficulty to strengthen our faith. This present suffering is not the last word in the story. Judgement will come for the oppressors. The saints will be with Christ forever.

Christians are suffering for their faith on this day all across our world. How can we who are not suffering today, connect with, help and encourage those who are bearing the costs of their faith?

COLLECT

O Lord Jesus Christ,
who at your first coming sent your messenger
to prepare your way before you:
grant that the ministers and stewards of your mysteries
may likewise so prepare and make ready your way
by turning the hearts of the disobedient to the wisdom of the just,
that at your second coming to judge the world
we may be found an acceptable people in your sight;
for you are alive and reign with the Father
in the unity of the Holy Spirit,
one God, now and for ever.

Reflection by **Steven Croft**

Psalms **76**, 97 *or* 56, **57** (63*)
Isaiah 51.9-16
2 Thessalonians 2

2 Thessalonians 2

'As to the coming of our Lord Jesus Christ ...' (v.1)

Reports have reached Paul and his companions that the Thessalonians are alarmed and shaken. The early Church believed that the coming of Christ was imminent. The Church therefore took very seriously the calls in the Gospels and the Epistles to keep awake.

There were some dangers as well, however. It was all too easy to be disturbed by rumours or false teaching that the coming of Christ as king had happened already and that the Thessalonians had been left behind and missed the kingdom.

Paul here seeks to counter these ideas and offer reassurance. He does so by a complex argument about a rebellion and a lawless one. This rebellion, Paul argues, must come first and therefore Christ has not yet returned. In other words, things are going to get much worse before they get better…

This imagery of the lawless one is complex. It builds on references in Daniel and other apocalyptic literature and is referenced again in the Gospels and Revelation. It is puzzling language for us today.

We need to remember that we live in a Church where the coming of Christ all too often does not seem imminent. Passages such as this challenge us to return to the creeds and remind one another that Christ will come again and that we too are called to keep awake.

God for whom we watch and wait,
you sent John the Baptist to prepare the way of your Son:
give us courage to speak the truth,
to hunger for justice,
and to suffer for the cause of right,
with Jesus Christ our Lord.

COLLECT

2 Thessalonians 3

'... keep away from believers who are living in idleness' (v.6)

Paul has addressed his first two themes of persecution and the timing of the coming of Christ. He now turns to the third report that has reached him: idleness in the Christian community.

The Church is called on in every generation to exercise mutual love and support and the practical sharing of goods. A strong work ethic is a necessary part of this culture of care for the poor. Without it, there is a danger of laziness and creating dependency. The kindness of Christian friends will be exploited by some, and the whole system of care will fall.

Most Christians finding time to read Paul's words in mid-December will probably raise their eyebrows at this point. The demands of family and working life and the extra demands of the season will probably mean there is too much to do and too little time to rest, let alone for idleness.

But there is a message here, even so, about the God-given importance of work, about the ingredients for human flourishing and about the way we build up our common life and responsibility: mutual care is not to be at the expense of individual dignity.

Everyone matters. Everyone's contribution matters. And that means your work and mine must be taken seriously today in itself and for the example we offer.

COLLECT

O Lord Jesus Christ,
who at your first coming sent your messenger
to prepare your way before you:
grant that the ministers and stewards of your mysteries
may likewise so prepare and make ready your way
by turning the hearts of the disobedient to the wisdom of the just,
that at your second coming to judge the world
we may be found an acceptable people in your sight;
for you are alive and reign with the Father
in the unity of the Holy Spirit,
one God, now and for ever.

Reflection by **Steven Croft**

Saturday 17 December

Jude

'Now to him who is able to keep you from falling...' (v.24)

The Letter of Jude is a sandwich. The bread is quite thin but full of goodness. The beginning of the letter (vv.1-2) and the end (vv.20-25) contain striking descriptions of the Church, a beautiful statement of priorities and one of the most profound prayers of blessing in the New Testament, often used in funeral services.

The filling in the sandwich is a long diatribe and a call to arms against the false teachers who rise up in every generation to trouble the Church. In Jude, these false teachers are particularly linked with sexual immorality of various kinds: their actions give them away. The letter chastises them piling up images from the Old Testament and the Apocrypha, mixing in metaphors from the natural world, adding, it seems, every insult under the sun.

We do need to remember in every generation to be discerning about those who are given influence over the Church. We need to look at the fruits of their lives and to be mindful of the dangers of false teachers.

But our main nourishment this day is likely to come from the bread rather than the filling in this particular sandwich. Think again on God's goodness this day. God has called you, God loves you deeply, God will keep you safe for Jesus Christ. God is able to keep us from falling. God is our Saviour. To him be the glory now and for ever.

God for whom we watch and wait,
you sent John the Baptist to prepare the way of your Son:
give us courage to speak the truth,
to hunger for justice,
and to suffer for the cause of right,
with Jesus Christ our Lord.

COLLECT

Reflection by **Steven Croft**   27

Monday 19 December

Psalms 144, **146**
Isaiah 52.13 – end of 53
2 Peter 1.1-15

2 Peter 1.1-15

'I intend to keep on reminding you of these things' (v.12)

All of us are formed by our long habits over time. Christian character emerges as God's grace works within us and as we respond to God's grace.

The author of 2 Peter knows that very little time is left to him (v.14). Death is not far away now. He uses what may be his final letter to the Church for reminding and re-member-ing. To re-member is, literally, to put things back together again: to reassemble the big picture of our faith, to re-orientate our lives again with God's love and grace and God's call at the centre.

It is easy at this time of year to be impatient with the Christmas season and the festivities. But at the very heart of Christmas and the celebration of the Church's year is this very act of remembering: rehearsing year by year in seasonal rhythms the great truths of our faith that lie at the heart of who we are and the people God calls us to be.

Even if our society ignored what we were doing, we would still celebrate the incarnation and Christmas. Surely we need to give thanks and rejoice that the whole world wants in some way to mark this season with us, to listen to the Christmas story, and to rehearse and remember this part of Christian truth.

COLLECT

God our redeemer,
who prepared the Blessed Virgin Mary
to be the mother of your Son:
grant that, as she looked for his coming as our saviour,
so we may be ready to greet him
when he comes again as our judge;
who is alive and reigns with you,
in the unity of the Holy Spirit,
one God, now and for ever.

Tuesday 20 December

2 Peter 1.16 – 2.3

'... eyewitnesses of his majesty' (1.16)

Peter reminds us of two of the great strands of truth that established the Christian faith in the first century and which see it re-established in every generation. We need to be as mindful of them today and pass them on to others.

The first is the witness of real events of history in the life of Jesus of Nazareth. The stories in the Gospels, the events we retell year by year, actually took place in a specific place and time. Real witnesses wrote down what they saw and what they heard and bore testimony to the truth. In these verses Peter describes again the transfiguration, the vision of Christ's glory given on the mountain (see Mark 9.2-8).

The second is witness of prophecy, of Scripture, fulfilled in Christ. Jesus' coming is foretold. This fulfilment of prophecy in the details of Jesus' life, death and resurrection confirms him as the Messiah and confirms the truth of our faith. The prophecy of Scripture fulfilled also gives us the interpretation and meaning of his ministry and his saving death.

God has spoken to us and speaks to us by the prophets and also by a Son (Hebrews 1.1-2). In this present darkness, and especially in our own times of darkness and difficulty, these are truths to anchor us, a lamp to guide us, burning bright until the dawn.

COLLECT

Eternal God,
as Mary waited for the birth of your Son,
so we wait for his coming in glory;
bring us through the birth pangs of this present age
to see, with her, our great salvation
in Jesus Christ our Lord.

Reflection by **Steven Croft**   29

Wednesday 21 December

2 Peter 2.4-end

'These are waterless springs and mists driven by a storm' (v.17)

The Church was not born in a century of peace and tranquility; the Church was born in century of conflict, persecution and contention. There was a raging market of ideas, a massive public debate about truth, and many different and competing views of the world.

The early Christians not only had to contend with the Roman state, which from time to time would persecute them; they also faced opposition in every city from the synagogues, who saw them as a deviant sect of Judaism. In addition, there were also other new religious movements, often disguised as false versions of the Christian faith, put forward by those who had been members of the Church.

Peter has these corrupt teachers in his sights here. Evidently, these are people who interpret freedom in Christ as freedom to do anything, including engaging in all kinds of sexual immorality. They are corrupting those who have been part of the Church and drawing them away for their own purposes.

Peter is writing, of course, before the Church had a settled canon of scripture, a stable ministry and a recognized pattern of oversight. All of these would emerge in the following generation as the apostles and eyewitnesses died. But his words (and Church history) remind us still of the need for vigilance against corrupted teaching in every generation.

COLLECT

God our redeemer,
who prepared the Blessed Virgin Mary
to be the mother of your Son:
grant that, as she looked for his coming as our saviour,
so we may be ready to greet him
when he comes again as our judge;
who is alive and reigns with you,
in the unity of the Holy Spirit,
one God, now and for ever.

Reflection by **Steven Croft**

2 Peter 3

'… what sort of people ought you to be?' (v.11)

One of the pressures on the first Christians was this: the first generation believed, very naturally, that the Lord would return very soon, put an end to suffering and establish the kingdom.

People from the new religions and the old mocked this belief that Christ would return as year after year went by. The apostles counter this mockery with a constant emphasis on true Christian hope: a steadfast assurance that Christ will return, at an hour we do not know and in God's own time.

Peter makes a distinctive contribution to this teaching in verses 8-9 with his assurance that for the Lord of heaven and earth, time moves differently. The delay is not because the Lord is slow but because the Lord is patient. A key element in his patience is love: he is not willing for anyone to perish, but for all to come to repentance.

The answering of one question leads, of course, to another. If the Lord is not to return yet for many years, how then should we wait and live and make the most of the time? A new ethic is needed. This question is answered not with a list of what we should do, but with a description of what kind of people we should be: leading lives of holiness and godliness.

As you come to the end of Advent, what kind of person have you been?

COLLECT

Eternal God,
as Mary waited for the birth of your Son,
so we wait for his coming in glory;
bring us through the birth pangs of this present age
to see, with her, our great salvation
in Jesus Christ our Lord.

Reflection by **Steven Croft** 31

Friday 23 December

2 John

'... so that our joy may be complete' (v.12)

Truth and love, fulfilment, joy and abiding are major themes of all of the Johannine writings in the New Testament. Here, they are skillfully woven together once more in this short letter to the elect lady, a picture of the Church of Jesus Christ.

Short letters say things in ways that longer letters do not. We come here straight to the heart of the matter: the heart of what it means to be the Church is to love one another. That love must be consistent with all of God's commandments – a call to walk in holiness.

But the letter is clear also about another truth, one that is very relevant at this time of the year when Christians will travel the length and breadth of the country to have contact with those they love. It is good to write and send texts and tweets and messages of all kinds, but it is even better to come and visit, to talk face to face. In that way our joy is made complete.

What better time of year to make these visits, to come and talk with friends face to face than the end of Advent and the beginning of Christmas. For this is the season when we remember, above all seasons, that God does not simply write to us or send us messages through others. God takes flesh and comes to live among us, meeting us face to face, so that our joy may be complete.

COLLECT

God our redeemer,
who prepared the Blessed Virgin Mary
to be the mother of your Son:
grant that, as she looked for his coming as our saviour,
so we may be ready to greet him
when he comes again as our judge;
who is alive and reigns with you,
in the unity of the Holy Spirit,
one God, now and for ever.

Reflection by **Steven Croft**

Psalms **45**, 113
Isaiah 58
3 John

3 John

'... he refuses to welcome the friends' (v.10)

How appropriate to read a reminder of the importance of hospitality on Christmas Eve. The Christmas story is full of hospitality and welcome: of people travelling to unfamiliar places on long journeys.

In these next days, as we celebrate Christ's birth, many of us will give and receive hospitality to friends and family and also, perhaps, to strangers or those we know less well. Good hospitality begins in the heart: in openness and generosity. It continues with a desire to bless others.

The Rule of Benedict says that guests are to be received as Christ (Benedict 53 quoting Matthew 25.35). They are to be met 'with every ceremony of love' and with humility and grace. All kindness is to be shown to them, and they are to be the first charge on the community while they are here.

Extended families as well as the Christian community are sustained and built up through hospitality. Patterns of welcome and generosity are established in this season and overflow in many different ways throughout the year.

So take time on this Christmas Eve to give thanks to God for the hospitality and welcome you will receive in the coming days. And take time to reflect for a moment on how you will extend that welcome to others.

Almighty God,
you make us glad with the yearly remembrance
of the birth of your Son Jesus Christ:
grant that, as we joyfully receive him as our redeemer,
so we may with sure confidence behold him
when he shall come to be our judge;
who is alive and reigns with you,
in the unity of the Holy Spirit,
one God, now and for ever.

COLLECT

Reflection by **Steven Croft** | 33

Morning Prayer – a simple form

Preparation

O Lord, open our lips
and our mouth shall proclaim your praise.

A prayer of thanksgiving for Advent

Blessed are you, Sovereign God of all,
to you be praise and glory for ever.
In your tender compassion
the dawn from on high is breaking upon us
to dispel the lingering shadows of night.
As we look for your coming among us this day,
open our eyes to behold your presence
and strengthen our hands to do your will,
that the world may rejoice and give you praise.
Blessed be God, Father, Son and Holy Spirit.
Blessed be God for ever.

Word of God

Psalmody *(the psalm or psalms listed for the day)*

**Glory to the Father and to the Son
and to the Holy Spirit;
as it was in the beginning is now:
and shall be for ever. Amen.**

Reading from Holy Scripture *(one or both of the passages set for the day)*

Reflection

The Benedictus (The Song of Zechariah) *(see opposite page)*

Prayers

Intercessions – a time of prayer for the day and its tasks, the world and its need, the church and her life.

The Collect for the Day

The Lord's Prayer *(see p. 37)*

Conclusion

A blessing or the Grace *(see p. 37)*, or a concluding response

Let us bless the Lord
Thanks be to God

Benedictus (The Song of Zechariah)

1   Blessed be the Lord the God of Israel, ♦
    who has come to his people and set them free.

2   He has raised up for us a mighty Saviour, ♦
    born of the house of his servant David.

3   Through his holy prophets God promised of old ♦
    to save us from our enemies,
       from the hands of all that hate us,

4   To show mercy to our ancestors, ♦
    and to remember his holy covenant.

5   This was the oath God swore to our father Abraham: ♦
    to set us free from the hands of our enemies,

6   Free to worship him without fear, ♦
    holy and righteous in his sight
       all the days of our life.

7   And you, child, shall be called the prophet of the Most High, ♦
    for you will go before the Lord to prepare his way,

8   To give his people knowledge of salvation ♦
    by the forgiveness of all their sins.

9   In the tender compassion of our God ♦
    the dawn from on high shall break upon us,

10 To shine on those who dwell in darkness
       and the shadow of death, ♦
    and to guide our feet into the way of peace.

Luke 1.68-79

**Glory to the Father and to the Son
and to the Holy Spirit;
as it was in the beginning is now:
and shall be for ever. Amen.**

Seasonal Prayers of Thanksgiving

Advent

Blessed are you, Sovereign God of all,
to you be praise and glory for ever.
In your tender compassion
the dawn from on high is breaking upon us
to dispel the lingering shadows of night.
As we look for your coming among us this day,
open our eyes to behold your presence
and strengthen our hands to do your will,
that the world may rejoice and give you praise.
Blessed be God, Father, Son and Holy Spirit.
Blessed be God for ever.

At Any Time

Blessed are you, creator of all,
to you be praise and glory for ever.
As your dawn renews the face of the earth
bringing light and life to all creation,
may we rejoice in this day you have made;
as we wake refreshed from the depths of sleep,
open our eyes to behold your presence
and strengthen our hands to do your will,
that the world may rejoice and give you praise.
Blessed be God, Father, Son and Holy Spirit.
Blessed be God for ever.

after Lancelot Andrewes (1626)

The Lord's Prayer and The Grace

Our Father in heaven,
hallowed be your name,
your kingdom come,
your will be done,
on earth as in heaven.
Give us today our daily bread.
Forgive us our sins
as we forgive those who sin against us.
Lead us not into temptation
but deliver us from evil.
For the kingdom, the power,
and the glory are yours
now and for ever.
Amen.

(or)

Our Father, who art in heaven,
hallowed be thy name;
thy kingdom come;
thy will be done;
on earth as it is in heaven.
Give us this day our daily bread.
And forgive us our trespasses,
as we forgive those who trespass against us.
And lead us not into temptation;
but deliver us from evil.
For thine is the kingdom,
the power and the glory,
for ever and ever.
Amen.

The grace of our Lord Jesus Christ,
and the love of God,
and the fellowship of the Holy Spirit,
be with us all evermore.
Amen.

An Order for Night Prayer (Compline)

Preparation

The Lord almighty grant us a quiet night and a perfect end.
Amen.

Our help is in the name of the Lord
who made heaven and earth.

A period of silence for reflection on the past day may follow.

The following or other suitable words of penitence may be used

Most merciful God,
we confess to you,
before the whole company of heaven and one another,
that we have sinned in thought, word and deed
and in what we have failed to do.
Forgive us our sins,
heal us by your Spirit
and raise us to new life in Christ. Amen.

O God, make speed to save us.
O Lord, make haste to help us.

Glory to the Father and to the Son
and to the Holy Spirit;
as it was in the beginning is now
and shall be for ever. Amen.
Alleluia.

The following or another suitable hymn may be sung

Before the ending of the day,
Creator of the world, we pray
That you, with steadfast love, would keep
Your watch around us while we sleep.

From evil dreams defend our sight,
From fears and terrors of the night;
Tread underfoot our deadly foe
That we no sinful thought may know.

O Father, that we ask be done
Through Jesus Christ, your only Son;
And Holy Spirit, by whose breath
Our souls are raised to life from death.

The Word of God

One or more of Psalms 4, 91 or 134 may be used.

Psalm 134

1   Come, bless the Lord, all you servants of the Lord, ♦
you that by night stand in the house of the Lord.

2   Lift up your hands towards the sanctuary ♦
and bless the Lord.

3   The Lord who made heaven and earth ♦
give you blessing out of Zion.

**Glory to the Father and to the Son
and to the Holy Spirit;
as it was in the beginning is now
and shall be for ever. Amen.**

Scripture Reading

*One of the following short lessons or another suitable
passage is read*

You, O Lord, are in the midst of us and we are called by your
name; leave us not, O Lord our God.

Jeremiah 14.9

(or)

Be sober, be vigilant, because your adversary the devil is
prowling round like a roaring lion, seeking for someone
to devour. Resist him, strong in the faith.

1 Peter 5.8,9

(or)

The servants of the Lamb shall see the face of God, whose name
will be on their foreheads. There will be no more night: they will
not need the light of a lamp or the light of the sun, for God will
be their light, and they will reign for ever and ever.

Revelation 22.4,5

Into your hands, O Lord, I commend my spirit.
Into your hands, O Lord, I commend my spirit.
For you have redeemed me, Lord God of truth.
I commend my spirit.
Glory to the Father and to the Son
and to the Holy Spirit.
Into your hands, O Lord, I commend my spirit.

Or, in Easter

Into your hands, O Lord, I commend my spirit.
    Alleluia, alleluia.
Into your hands, O Lord, I commend my spirit.
    Alleluia, alleluia.
For you have redeemed me, Lord God of truth.
Alleluia, alleluia.
Glory to the Father and to the Son
and to the Holy Spirit.
Into your hands, O Lord, I commend my spirit.
    Alleluia, alleluia.

Keep me as the apple of your eye.
Hide me under the shadow of your wings.

Gospel Canticle

Nunc Dimittis (The Song of Simeon)

Save us, O Lord, while waking,
and guard us while sleeping,
that awake we may watch with Christ
and asleep may rest in peace.

1   Now, Lord, you let your servant go in peace:
    your word has been fulfilled.

2   My own eyes have seen the salvation
    which you have prepared in the sight of every people;

3   A light to reveal you to the nations
    and the glory of your people Israel.

Luke 2.29-32

Glory to the Father and to the Son
and to the Holy Spirit;
as it was in the beginning is now
and shall be for ever. Amen.

Save us, O Lord, while waking,
and guard us while sleeping,
that awake we may watch with Christ
and asleep may rest in peace.

Prayers

Intercessions and thanksgivings may be offered here.

The Collect

Visit this place, O Lord, we pray,
and drive far from it the snares of the enemy;
may your holy angels dwell with us and guard us in peace,
and may your blessing be always upon us;
through Jesus Christ our Lord.
Amen.

The Lord's Prayer (see p. 37) may be said.

The Conclusion

In peace we will lie down and sleep;
for you alone, Lord, make us dwell in safety.

Abide with us, Lord Jesus,
for the night is at hand and the day is now past.

As the night watch looks for the morning,
so do we look for you, O Christ.

[Come with the dawning of the day
and make yourself known in the breaking of the bread.]

The Lord bless us and watch over us;
the Lord make his face shine upon us and be gracious to us;
the Lord look kindly on us and give us peace.
Amen.

Love what you've read?

Why not consider using *Reflections for Daily Prayer* all year round? We also publish these Bible reflections in an annual format, containing material for the entire church year.

The volume for the **2016/17** church year is now available and features contributions from a host of distinguished writers: Jeff Astley, Joanna Collicutt, Steven Croft, Jonathan Frost, Paula Gooder, Helen-Ann Hartley, Christopher Herbert, Graham James, Libby Lane, Barbara Mosse, Helen Orchard, John Perumbalath, John Pritchard, Sarah Rowland Jones, Tim Sledge, Angela Tilby and Margaret Whipp.

REFLECTIONS FOR DAILY PRAYER
Advent 2016 to the eve of Advent 2017

ISBN 978 0 7151 4715 3 • **£16.99**

Please note: this book reproduces the material for Advent found in the volume you are now holding.

Reflections for Daily Prayer **2017/18** will be available from May 2017 with reflections written by: Christopher Cocksworth, Gillian Cooper, Stephen Cottrell, Steven Croft, Maggi Dawn, Malcolm Guite, Christopher Herbert, John Kiddle, Barbara Mosse, Mark Oakley, Martyn Percy, John Pritchard, Ben Quash, Angela Tilby, Catherine Williams, Jane Williams, Lucy Winkett, Christopher Woods and Jeremy Worthen.

REFLECTIONS FOR DAILY PRAYER
Advent 2017 to the eve of Advent 2018

ISBN 978 1 78140 019 7
£16.99 • 336 pages

REFLECTIONS FOR DAILY PRAYER
App

Make Bible study and reflection a part of your routine wherever you go with the Reflections for Daily Prayer App for Apple and Android devices.

Download the app for free from the App Store (Apple devices) or Google Play (Android devices) and receive a week's worth of reflections free. Then purchase a monthly, three-monthly or annual subscription to receive up-to-date content.

REFLECTIONS FOR SUNDAYS (YEAR A)

Reflections for Sundays offers over 250 reflections on the Principal Readings for every Sunday and major Holy Day in Year A, from the same experienced team of writers that have made *Reflections for Daily Prayer* so successful. For each Sunday and major Holy Day, they provide:

- full lectionary details for the Principal Service
- a reflection on each Old Testament reading (both Continuous and Related)
- a reflection on the Epistle
- a reflection on the Gospel.

£14.99 • 288 pages
ISBN 978 0 7151 4735 1

This book also contains a substantial introduction to the Gospel of Matthew, written by Paula Gooder.

Also available in Kindle and epub formats

REFLECTIONS ON THE PSALMS

£14.99 • 192 pages
ISBN 978 0 7151 4490 9

Reflections on the Psalms provides original and insightful meditations on each of the Bible's 150 Psalms.

Each reflection is accompanied by its corresponding Psalm refrain and prayer from the *Common Worship Psalter*, making this a valuable resource for personal or devotional use.

Specially written introductions by Paula Gooder and Steven Croft explore the Psalms and the Bible and the Psalms in the life of the Church.